This **book** belongs to:

Hello!

Already as a child I began making prints with whatever fell into my hands: my fingers, stamps, potatoes, torn-off pants' buttons, and other found objects: nothing was safe around me!

I never lost this passion. When I was in college I travelled to Andalusia in Spain. There I found not only trees, flotsam and jetsam, and half a forest to use for printing, but also parts of a shipwreck. You can see one of the results of this in the whale's tailfin on the page to the left ...

In this book I'll show you how to make great prints using very simple means. You'll need only your own fingers, scraps of fruits and vegetables, and a couple of supplies. You can make prints with almost anything you can imagine: the sky's the limit. And you'll soon find out that once you get started, more and more fun ideas will occur to you.

Have fun printing!

Julia Kaergel

This is what you'll need to make prints:

stamp pads
in a variety of
colors and sizes

watercolors or gouache

in tubes or pans,
including opaque white

found objects

**VEGETABLES and
kitchen scraps**

**scraps of cardboard
stamps**

**your hands
your finger**

onions

rose hips

bell peppers

poppy capsules

paper
of different kinds:
colored, thick, thin, patterned,
anything you can find

a glass of water
a rag or paper **towels**

brushes to apply paint
to the objects or stamps

a brayer
to roll the paint onto an
old plate or an acrylic plate
(you can find these in
craft stores)

materials for drawing and painting

Scissors
glue
pencils
fineliner pens
inks
a small paring knife

ink

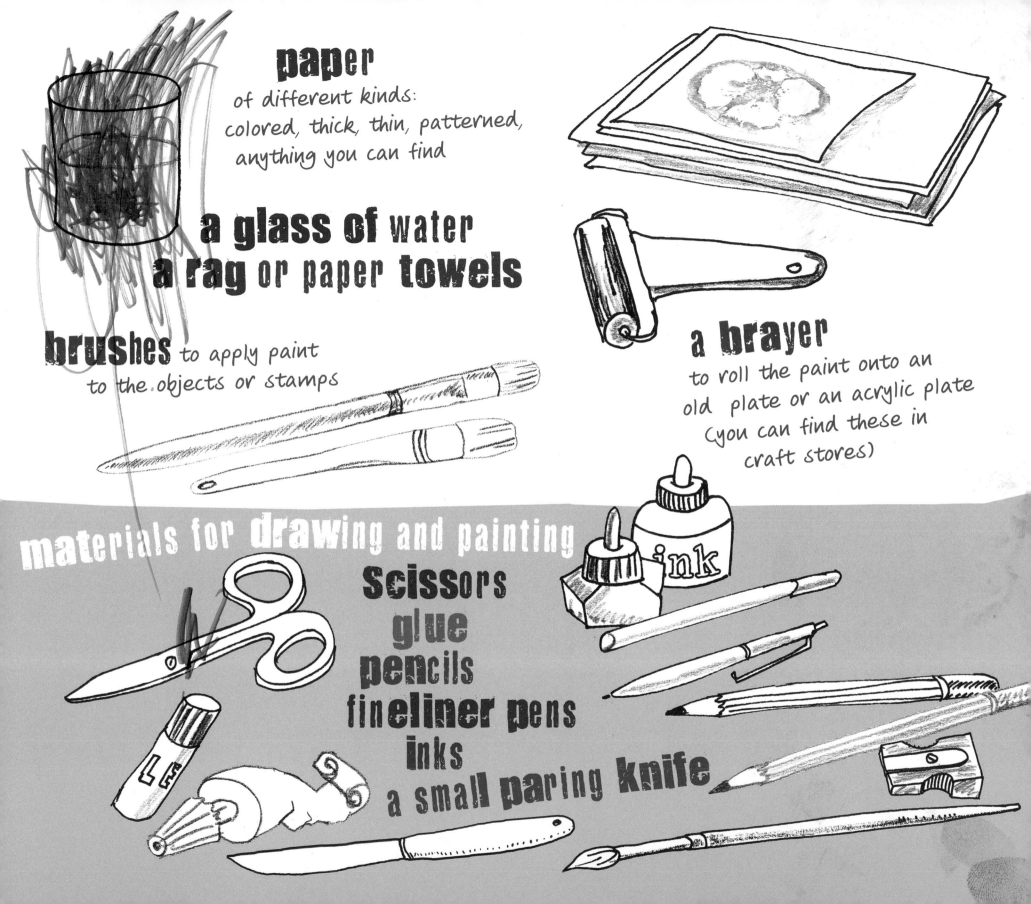

And here's **what to do:**

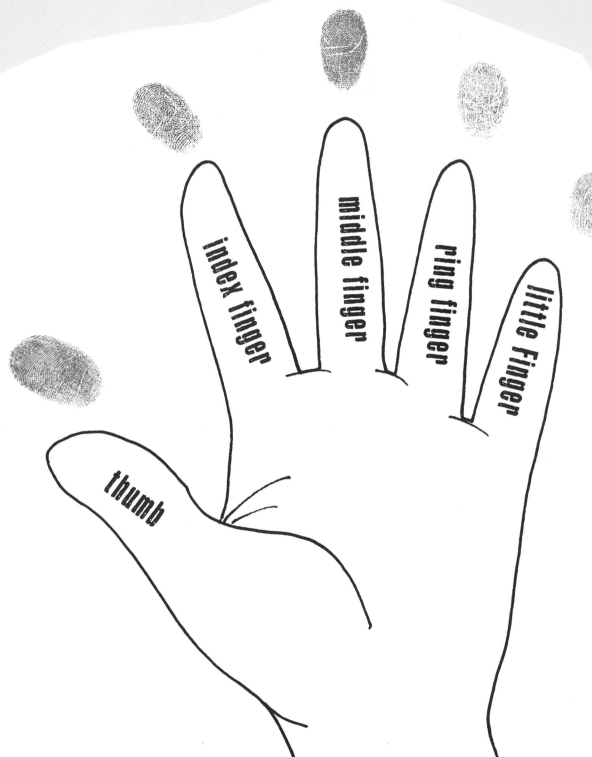

index finger

middle finger

ring finger

little Finger

thumb

Look: each finger makes
a different print.
Try it yourself.

It's probably best to
use one hand for printing
and the other for
drawing.

Try to keep the different
stamp pads clean by using
only one per finger. Or you
can wipe your finger with a
paper towel before using
another color.

1.

Press your finger onto a stamp pad or paint it with a paintbrush.

2.

Then press your finger onto a piece of paper.

3.

Let the impression dry.

4.

You can use a pencil, pen, or brush to make a little bird from your fingerprint.

Try **experimenting** with different forms and templates.

circle

only the tip of your finger

oval

one finger

half oval

a fingerprint over a piece of paper

triangle

a fingerprint over a stencil made of three pieces of paper

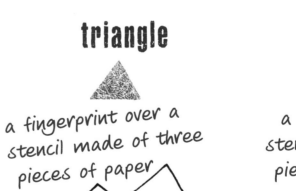

square

a fingerprint over a stencil made of four pieces of paper

And a partridge in a pear tree...

How many different kinds of birds can you draw?

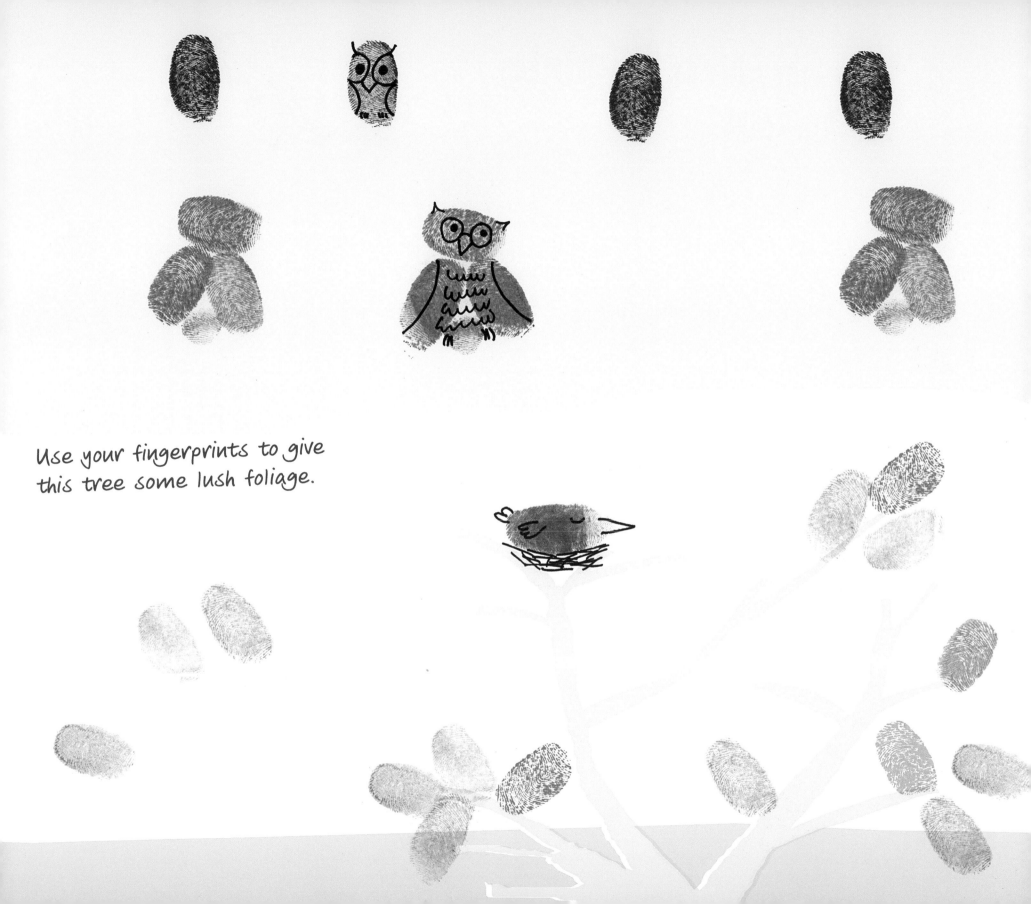

Use your fingerprints to give this tree some lush foliage.

How many birds are **hiding**
in the trees?

Tivili!

Who's flying and **crawling** around here?

Here's space for a lot of small **wild animals ...**

... and for **some bigger ones.**

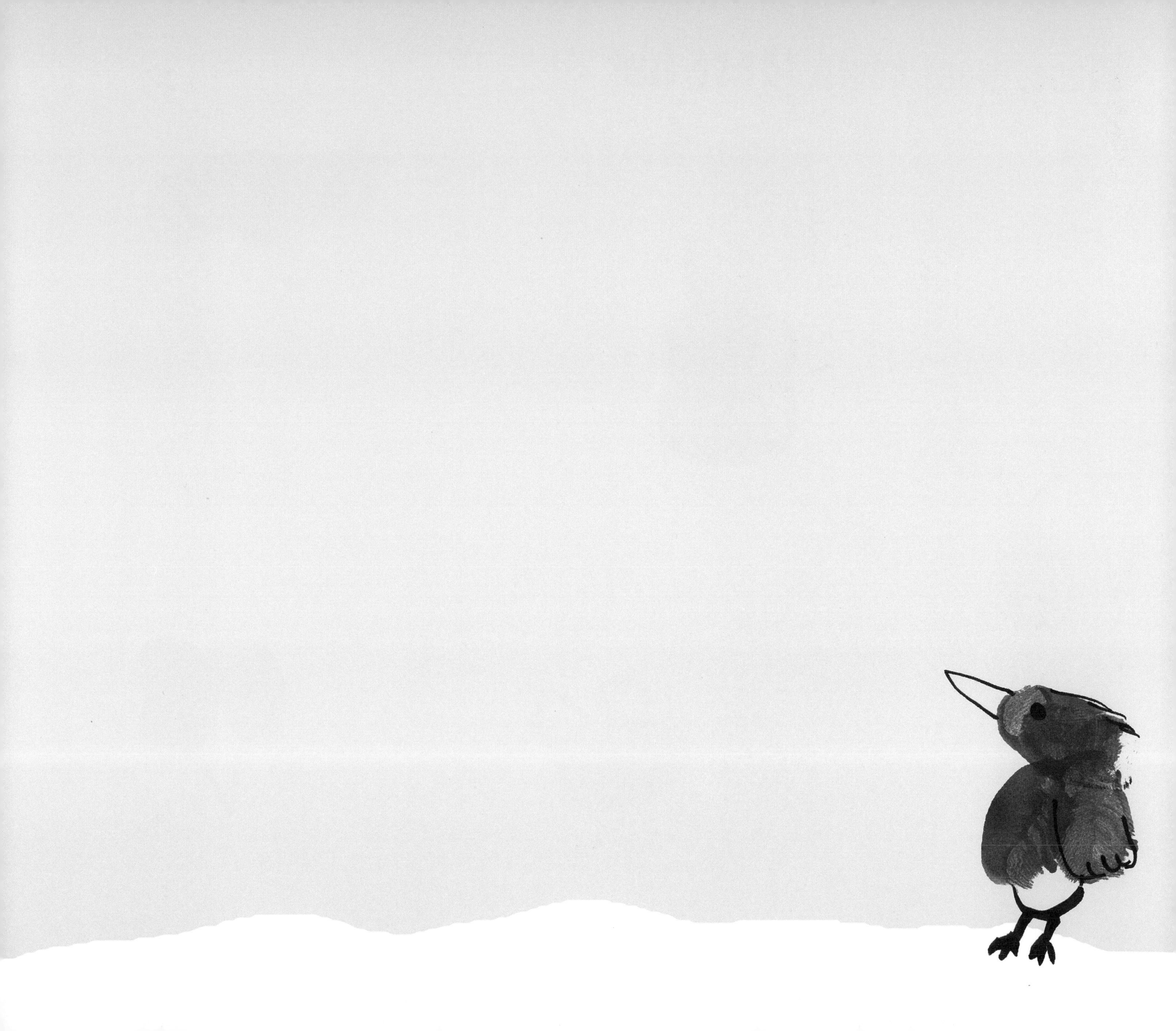

Whoa, what could these be?

Try making some prints with your whole hand.

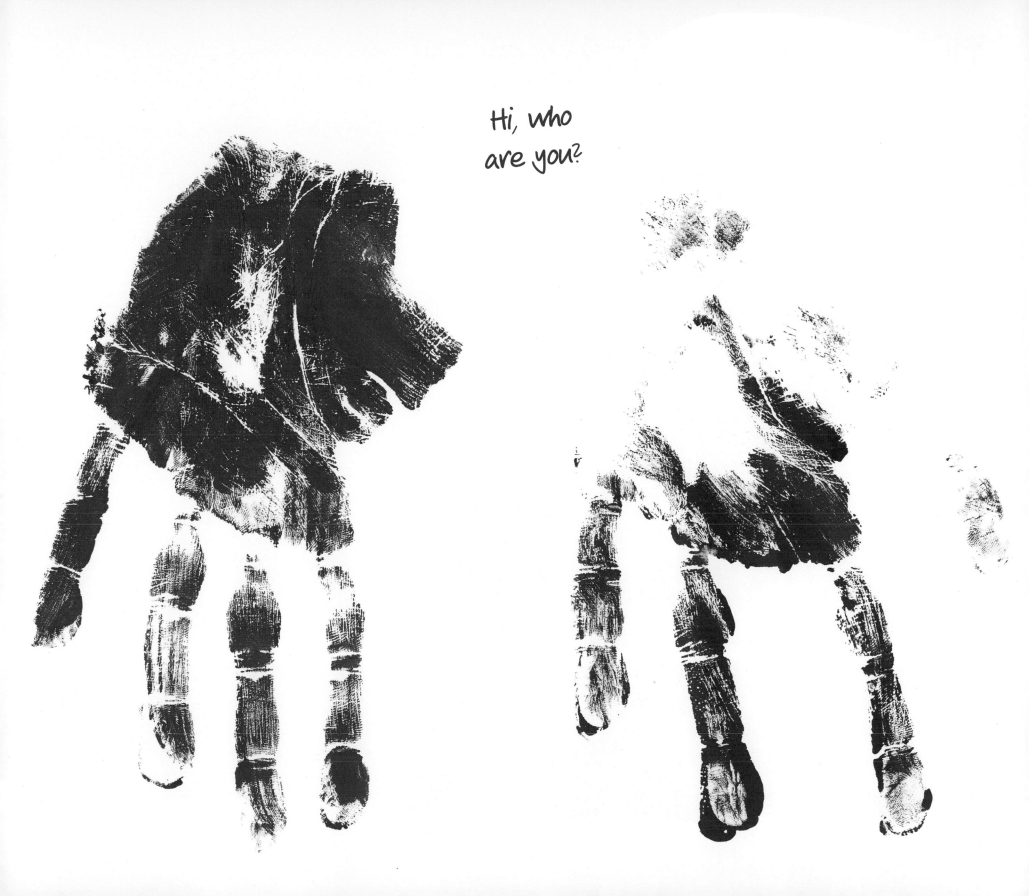

What's going on here?

Two foot-noseys having a conversation!

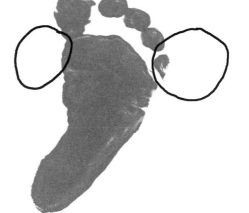

How big are your feet?

my flip-flop

You can make great **stamps with fruit** and **vegetables.**

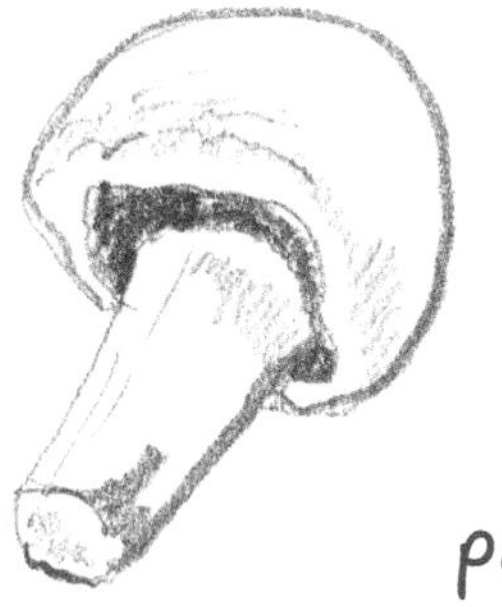

How about some experiments?

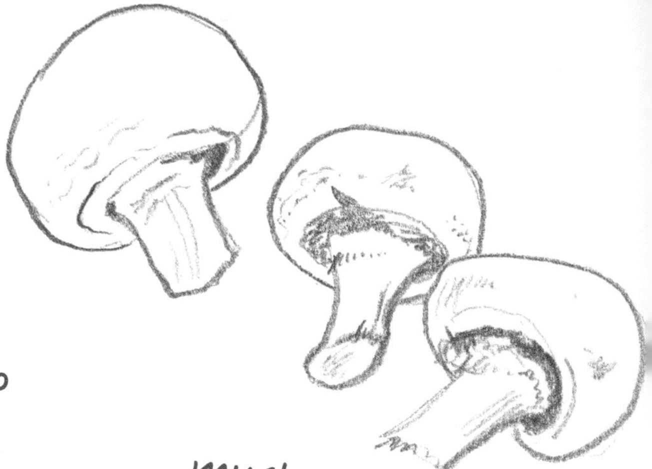

Cut a vegetable in half. Press it onto the stamp pad or use a brush to apply a layer of paint to it. Use lots of different colors.

mushrooms

Here goes...

broccoli

apple

What could be hiding in this deep, dark forest?

You can use mushrooms, broccoli, and an arborvitae branch to print a dark forest. What else could you use?

Vegetable scraps can make beautiful **flowers.**

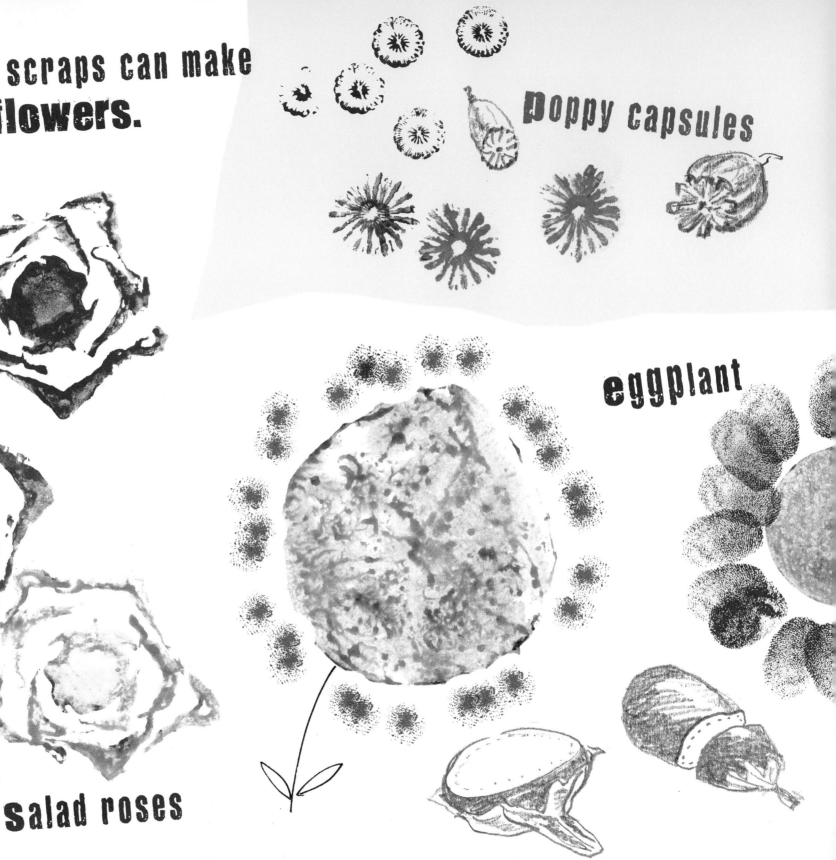

poppy capsules

eggplant

salad roses

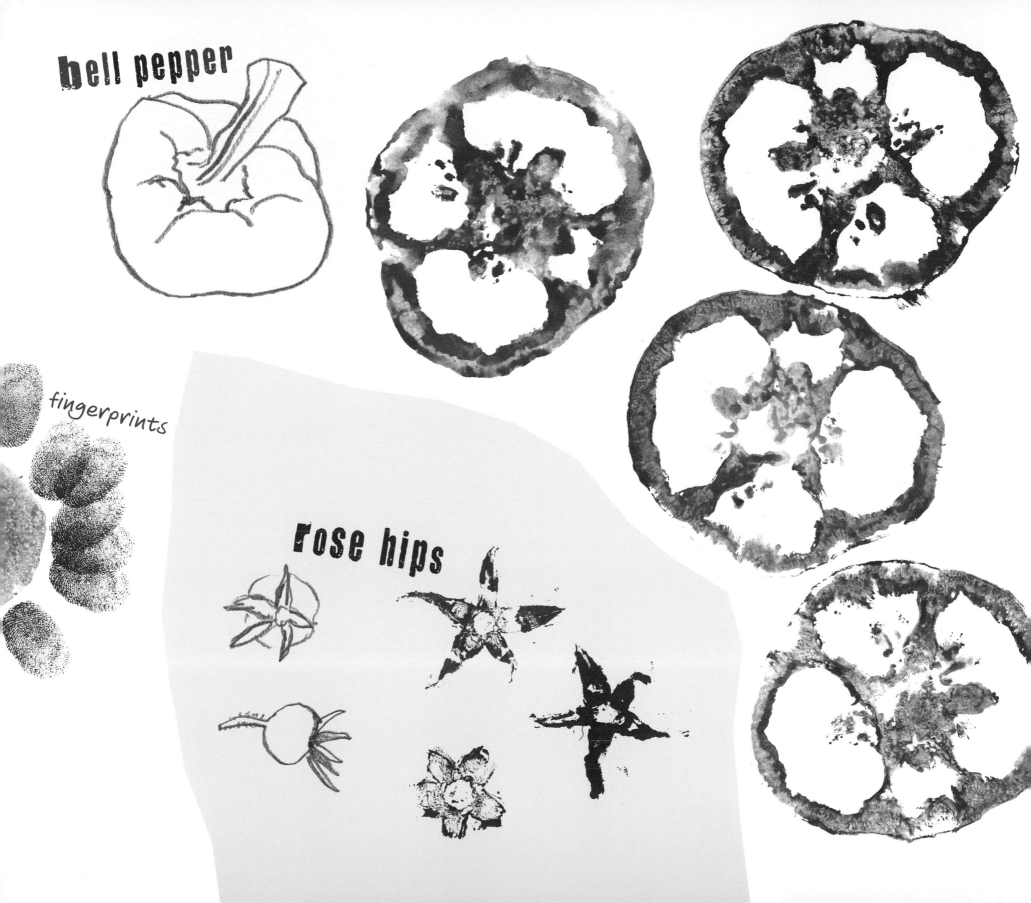

bell pepper

fingerprints

rose hips

What does yOur flower meadow look like?

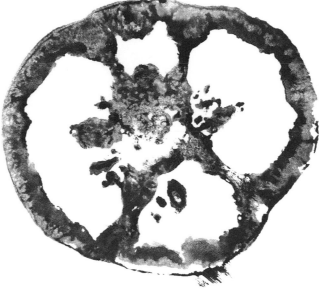

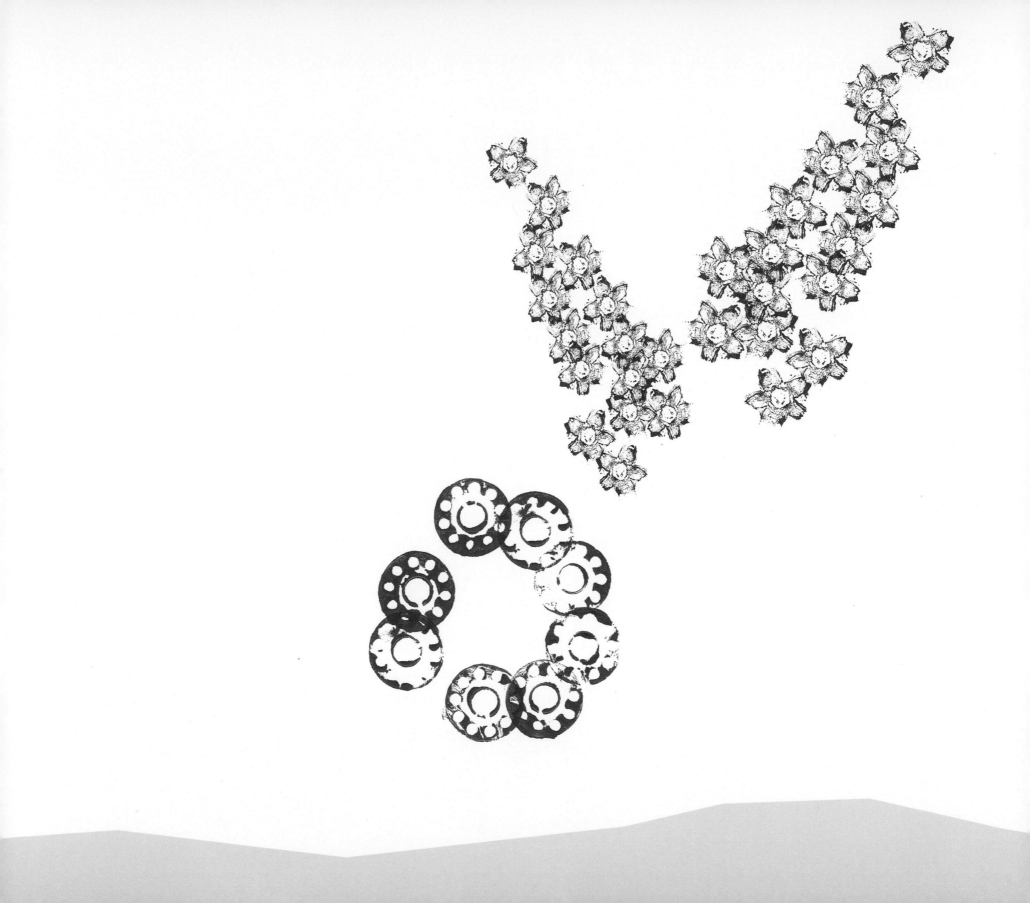

Do these beautiful flowers have a scent?

You can print flower petals with...

Onions

fennel

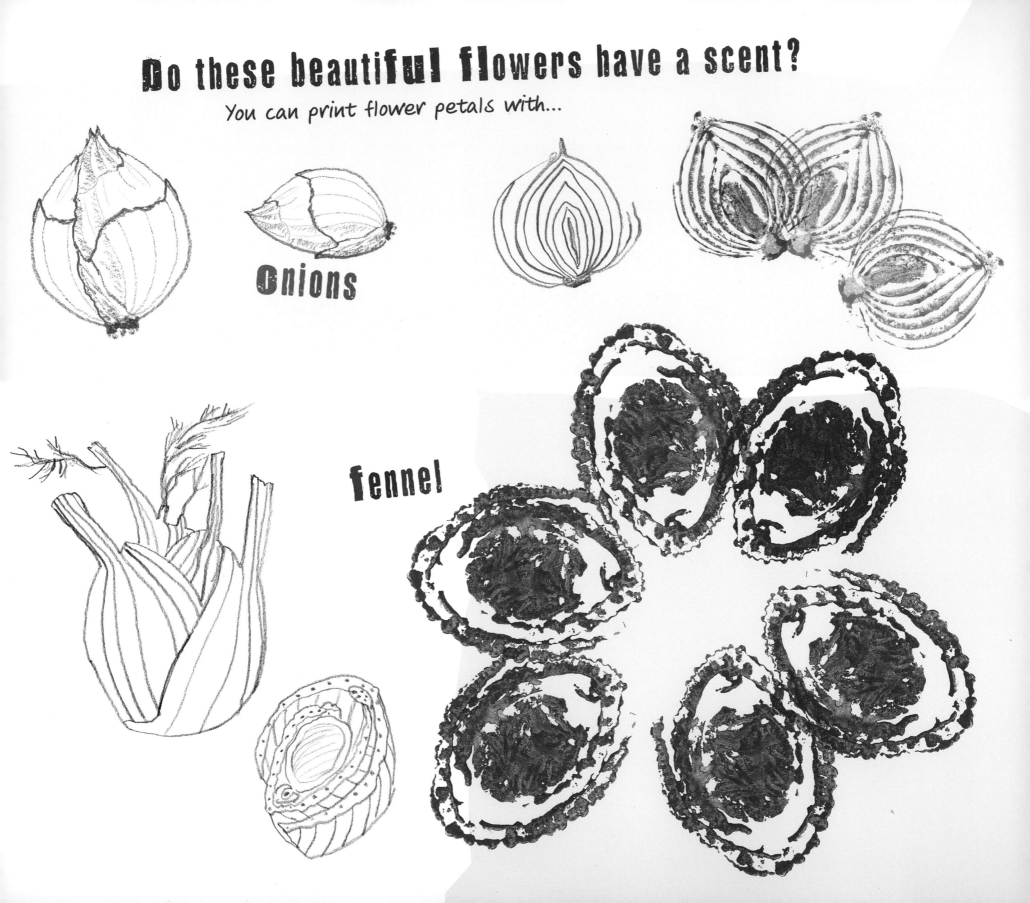

What's that?
A **mushroom!**

leeks

This bouquet is for ....

The wheels of the **potato car** go round and round...

doilies

sewing machine bobbins

buttons

a potato car

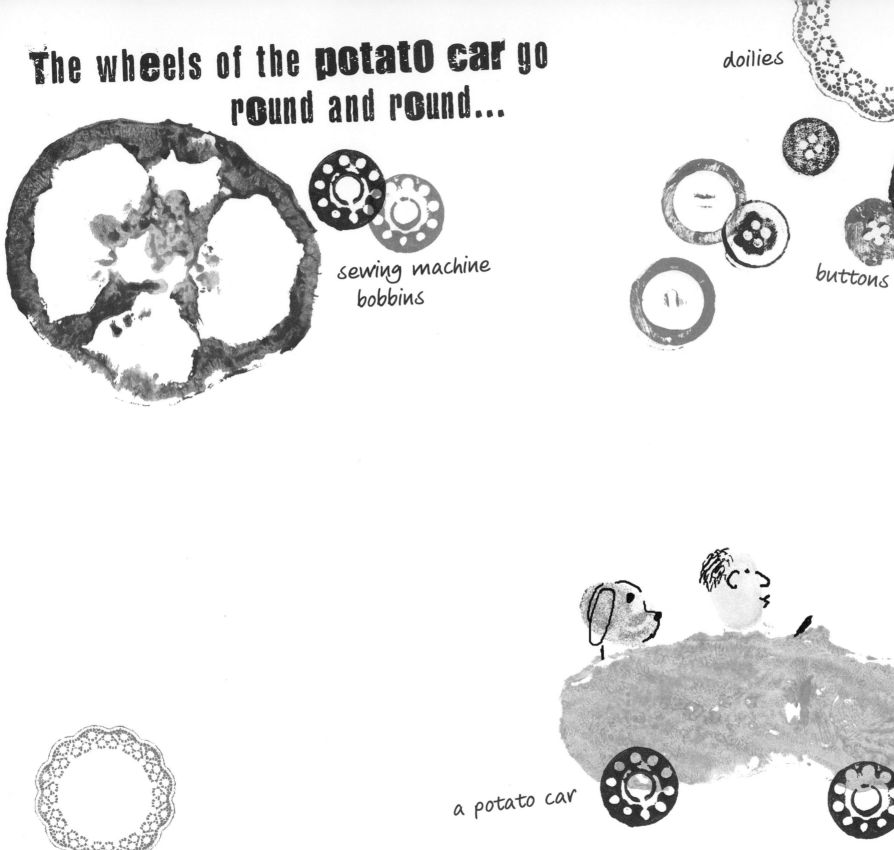

apple

potato

Downhill is fastER!

What are your favorite **foods**?

half a thumb

two thumbs

fingertips

a bundle of rubber bands

a whole finger

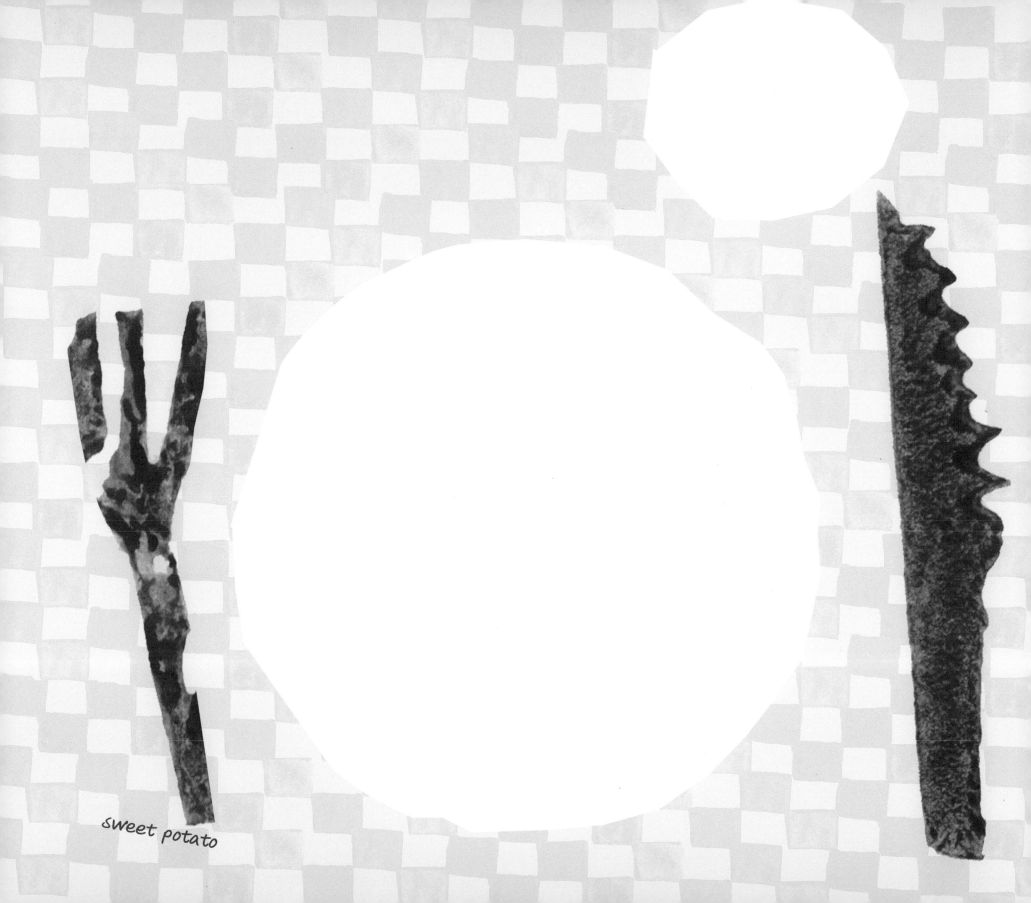

sweet potato

Foods I don't like at all:

How to make a **potato stAmp:**

First, cut the potatoes into halves, crosswise or lengthwise.

Then use a knife to score a design into the potato, about 1/8 inch deep.

Carefully carve around the shape you just made, using the knife to cut away the parts you don't want. To make a good print the design has to be higher than the cut-away parts.

Now dry the cut edge with a paper towel and your potato stamp is ready to use!

Don't forget: Your finished print will always be a mirror image of the stamp. With most designs that's no problem, but with some, like letters, it could be.

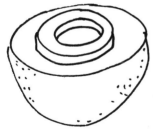

After a few days your printing block will shrivel up. Then it's time to make some new stamps.

Two circles can make eyes:

What are you looking at?

Here comes the pOtato alligator!

You can use your stamps over and over again.

Who's waiting for the alligatOr?

Funny people with cool **hair-dos.**

an ear of wheat

a scallion

a roll of
toilet paper

Contest for the most unusual costume

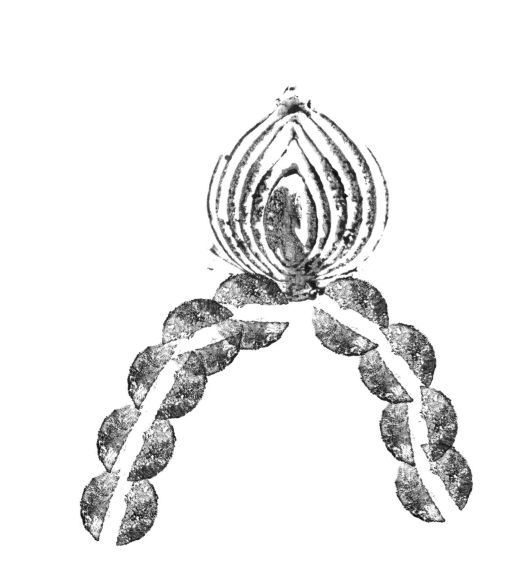

My family

Mom

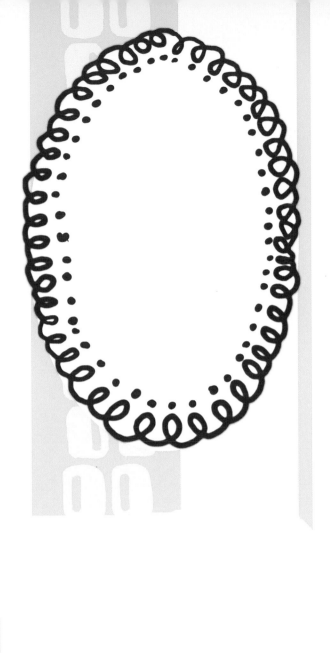

MasQUERade bAll

No one would recognize me like this.

When you make prints with red beets, you don't need paint or a stamp pad. The beet's red color is so intense that you can simply print it onto the paper directly. You might want to wear rubber gloves.

leek

rolled
lemon
peel

Who lives on this planet?

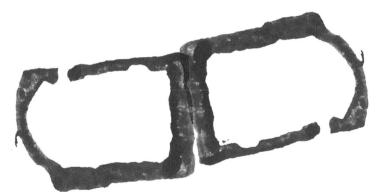

Can you guess what the
stamps were made from?
potato, onion, corks ...

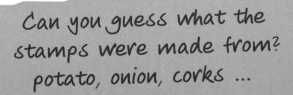

All the people on this planet are green!

These aliens glow in the **dark.**

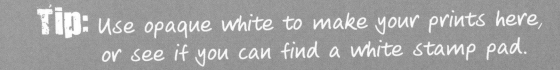

Tip: Use opaque white to make your prints here, or see if you can find a white stamp pad.

Who gets the bOne?

sweet potato

artichoke.

Where are you **flying?**

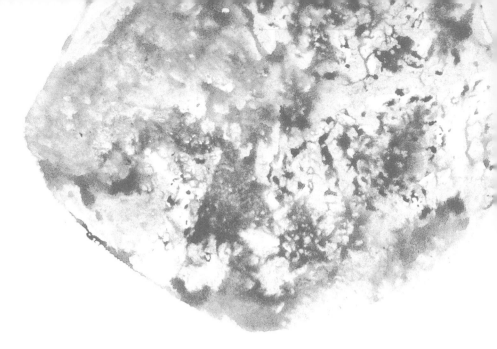

apple

This is what my **hometown** looks like from above.

It's called ....

Here you can find really good ....

pointed cabbage

Who lives in this big building?

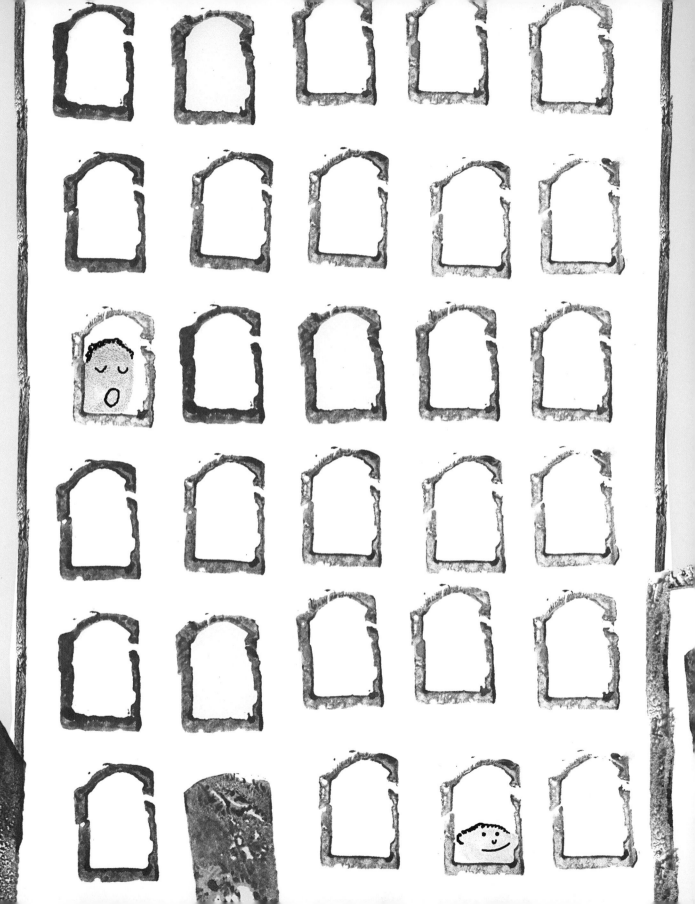

potato

potato prints

This is my dreAm house!

It's humming and **buzzing**...
Invent some new insects.

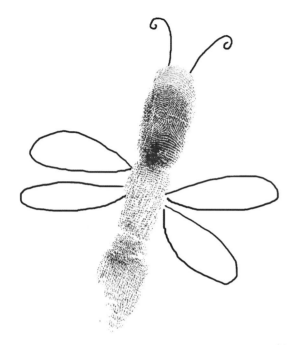

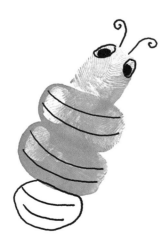

How many **mice** live in the **hole?**

sweet potato

Snail parade

apple

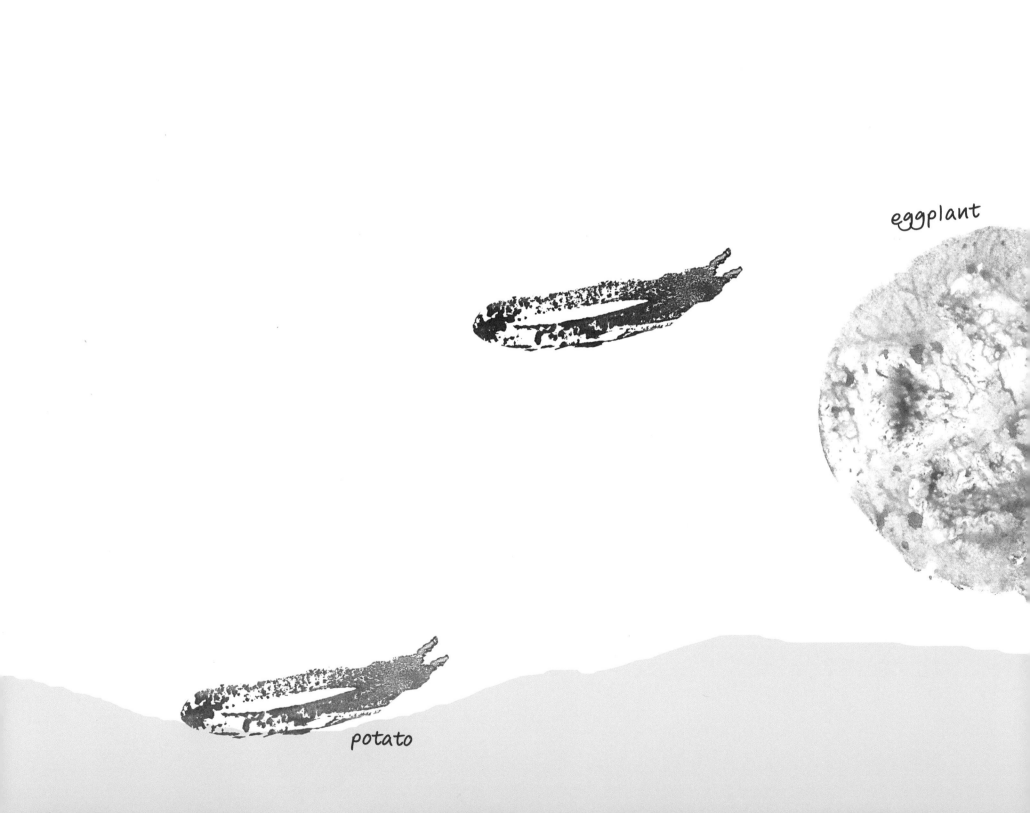

eggplant

potato

What's rUstling in the leaves?

flip-flop hedgehog

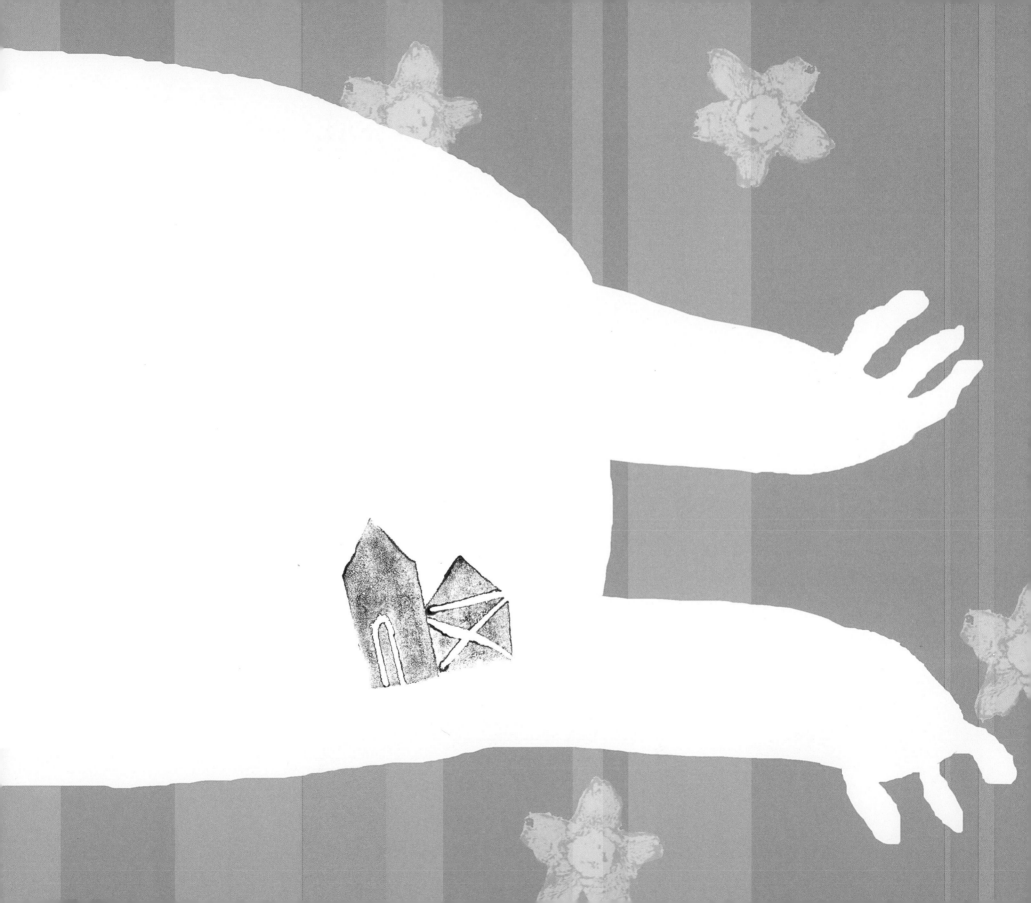

The moNSter's still hungry!

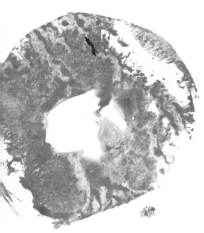

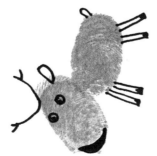

© Prestel Verlag, Munich · London · New York, 2013

Prestel Verlag, Munich
www.prestel.de

Prestel Publishing Ltd.
14-17 Wells Street
London W1T 3PD

Prestel Publishing
900 Broadway, Suite 603
New York, NY 10003

www.prestel.com

Prestel books are available worldwide. Please contact your nearest bookseller
or one of the above addresses for information concerning your local distributor.

Text, illustration, design and layout: Julia Kaergel
Translation and English copy-editing: Cynthia Hall
Production: Astrid Wedemeyer
Art direction: Cilly Klotz
Lithography: Reproline Mediateam, Munich
Printing and binding: Lanarepro GmbH, Lana

Verlagsgruppe Random House FSC®-N001967
The FSC®-certified paper Tauro has been
supplied by Papier Union.

MIX
Paper from
responsible sources
FSC® C016410
FSC
www.fsc.org

Printed in Italy

ISBN 978-3-7913-7142-9